THE RIGHT DEFENSE FOR A TRAFFIC OFFENSE IN VIRGINIA

ANDREW R. PAGE

WORD ASSOCIATION PUBLISHERS
www.wordassociation.com
1.800.827.7903

ISBN: 978-1-63385-406-2

Published by
Word Association Publishers
205 Fifth Avenue
Tarentum, Pennsylvania 15084

www.wordassociation.com
1.800.827.7903

CONTENTS

INTRODUCTION

YOU ARE DRIVING THROUGH VIRGINIA, LISTENING TO THE radio, when you hear a siren. You look in the rearview mirror and see flashing blue lights coming behind you. Immediately, you check the speedometer. Then you turn to see whether there are other cars around you. Once you understand the blue lights are for you, you slow down and pull over. The officer stops his patrol car behind your vehicle. He steps out and approaches your car. What do you say? How should you act? *Why me!*

You are not alone. Every day thousands of drivers are pulled over by Virginia police officers, sheriff deputies, and state troopers. Some Virginia cities and counties are more notorious for their traffic citations than others. But no matter where you are pulled over, you will no doubt feel uncertainty, anxiety, and, perhaps, even shame. Most people rarely go to court. It can be an intimidating excursion. Standing before the general public in front of a judge may feel daunting, especially when you do not know what to say or do.

This book is meant to help you with that. Having handled thousands of Virginia traffic cases in numerous courts over the past decade, I have written this book to help you prepare your case or learn how to find an experienced Virginia traffic attorney to help you with your ticket. If you cannot afford an attorney, this book will help you navigate the legal process of defending a traffic case (under the current law in Virginia – always check with an attorney concerning updates).

I will teach you how to conduct yourself at traffic stops to put yourself in the best possible position before the court. You will learn what to say to the judge and what evidence will help you make your case. But it is important to note that this book is for informational purposes only. It does not create an attorney-client relationship with the author, nor does it guarantee any specific outcome for you or replace the effectiveness that hiring an attorney can provide. Therefore, if at all possible, you should consider hiring an experienced traffic attorney for your case.

This book is backed not only with experience but by testimonials of satisfied clients. One client wrote, "Mr. Page handled a complicated traffic citation for our family with awesome results. The outcome was actually way better than we had hoped." The knowledge and advocacy skills I used to defend this client, and countless more, are contained in this small volume. If you read it and apply it, you will put yourself in the best possible position to fight your ticket.

CHAPTER 1

BE POLITE AND COOPERATIVE

WHEN SOMEONE CLAIMS THAT WE HAVE DONE something wrong, we tend to get defensive. We have to protect our honor and our good name. Therefore, we often argue and fight against claims of wrongdoing. Nowhere is this seen more than at traffic stops. Drivers mistakenly argue with the police officer, thinking that perhaps through their excellent debate skills the officer will see their point of view and change his or her mind about giving a citation. Some get angry and accuse the officer of having improper motives in the stop. But nothing could be more damaging to your case. The key to having a potentially good outcome in your traffic case is found in five words the judge will eventually ask: "Was he/she polite and cooperative?" If the officer answers with anything other than "Yes!" there will be little hope for a good result.

The answer to this question begins the moment the blue lights flash and the siren sounds. In Virginia, drivers are required to pull over immediately. Failure to pull over after being signaled to do so can result in bigger problems, such as a felony eluding charge. Requiring a law enforcement officer to risk his or her life driving at high speeds down the roads and endangering other drivers will make things even worse. **Just pull over.** Better a little pain than a world of hurt.

When the officer approaches the vehicle, comply with all lawful demands. Have your license and registration ready to turn over. Stay in your seat with your seatbelt on. Do not get out of the vehicle. Do not make any obscene gestures at the officer. Just get through the process as quickly and painlessly as possible by doing what you are required to do.

But to be clear, being polite and cooperative does not require you to answer any of the officer's questions. You have a constitutional right to remain silent. Anything you say can, and will be, used against you in court. So if the officer asks, "Do you know how fast you were going?" and you respond, "Yes, I know I was speeding," you can be sure the officer will repeat that statement to the judge. If an officer asks you that question, you can say, "Officer, I politely and cooperatively decline to answer any questions without a lawyer present." You do not need to assert your rights in some haughty or abrupt manner. Simply make a statement, such as the one provided, and the officer must cease communications. You can expect that you will still get a ticket, but at least you have preserved your defenses for court.

So why should I not talk to the officer about my case if I do not think I am guilty? There are several reasons. First, it is unlikely that you will talk yourself out of getting a ticket regardless. The officer did not pull you without a reason. It is unlikely that you are such a skilled debater that you will convince the officer that he or she made a mistake in pulling you over. Second, even if you think you were going a lawful speed, and you tell the officer you were going that speed, now your testimony has been set. So when the judge asks the officer what happened, the officer will respond, "I clocked the Defendant going X speed. When I asked the Defendant how fast she was going, she said she was going Y speed." Now you are in a credibility match with the officer. These officers regularly appear before these judges. Who do you think will be viewed as credible and who will be judged as having lied?

Third, if you are charged with a citation due to an accident, your statement may be the only one that is able to convict you. In several reckless driving accident cases I have defended, the officer appeared but the victim of the crash did not. If the Defendant does not speak to the officer, and the officer did not observe the crash itself, the judge would have to dismiss the case. But where a Defendant told the officer that he was going too fast or was not paying attention, and the victim did not appear, the officer can simply tell the judge what the Defendant admitted. As a result, the judge says, "Guilty!" There really is no good reason to talk to the police about your case without a lawyer.

Though you should assert your rights, you should do so in a polite and cooperative manner. In almost every case where the Defendant is polite and cooperative to the officer, the judge gives the Defendant some sort of break. But in almost every case where the Defendant is rude or uncooperative with the police, the judge drops the hammer! Being polite and cooperative is the first step in setting up a successful outcome for your traffic offense.

CHAPTER 2

KNOW YOUR CHARGE

THE OFFICER HAS TAKEN YOUR LICENSE AND registration to his car. After sitting several minutes, the officer comes back and hands you your license, registration, and a piece of paper. If it is a ticket for an infraction, the officer will advise you that you can sign acknowledging you do not have to appear in court. If it is a misdemeanor charge, you will not be given that option. So how do you know what infraction or misdemeanor you are charged with?

Virginia has a plethora of traffic offenses in the Virginia Code. In order for you to be found guilty, the officer has to put the code section that you violated on the piece of paper he gave you. If you cannot make out the scribble, you can look up your charge on the Virginia Judicial System website. Click on Online Case Information System-Statewide Search and plug in your information. You will find lots of important information there, such as your ticket code section, whether it is an infraction or misdemeanor, the officer's last name, and your court date. Once you see the code section you are charged with, you can do a Google search for "Virginia Code Section _____."

Whether a charge is a traffic infraction or misdemeanor can sometimes be tricky. For example, a person can be charged with misdemeanor reckless driving in Virginia for driving any speed twenty or more miles per hour over the speed limit or any speed over eighty-five miles per hour (under current Virginia Code Section 46.2-862). No additional reckless conduct is needed for this charge to stick. But an officer can, in the officer's discretion, write the ticket for simple speeding twenty or more over or over eighty-five miles per hour. Needless to say, there are more options within your grasp for a charge written as speeding that may not be there for a misdemeanor reckless driving charge. Similarly, Virginia has a failure to yield infraction charge and a failure to yield reckless driving charge. Knowing what Virginia Code Section you are charged with is crucial to your defense.

Once you know the Virginia Code Section of your charge, you may enhance your defense by looking for Virginia Supreme Court and Virginia Court of Appeals cases regarding your offense. Suppose you are charged with reckless driving generally under Virginia Code Section 46.2-852 as a result of an accident. The officer did not observe the crash and you did not make any statement to the officer (Good job for listening to my earlier suggestion!). You search for Virginia Supreme Court cases involving reckless driving and accidents.

In your search, you stumble upon *Powers v. Commonwealth*, decided in 1970. In that case, the Commonwealth argued that a driver was reckless where he traveled erratically for over 900 feet and hit a tree so hard the motor wrenched from it the car. The court, however, disagreed. The court held that an accident alone does not give rise to an inference of reckless driving. With that information, do you think your reckless driving defense will be made stronger? You bet. The Virginia Supreme Court is the Commonwealth's highest court. It serves as binding precedent on all lower courts, including the Virginia General and Juvenile and Domestic Relations District Courts. If an officer tries to reconstruct your accident that the officer did not observe, and there are no other witnesses, this case can serve as reason to object to the officer's testimony and give grounds to make a motion to strike (which is the Virginia equivalent of a motion to dismiss).

If you are going to rely on case law, it is important to ensure that the case is still good law. While *Powers* is currently good law, the Virginia Supreme Court can decide a case later on that reverses that case. So if the Supreme Court has overturned a past case, you would look ignorant waving an outdated case in front of the judge. This point is reason enough to hire an attorney, rather than attempt to represent yourself. It takes a lot of time to ensure that case law is still valid, and it can be frustrating to attempt if you have no experience doing it. But if you are going to represent yourself, you must follow this step.

To prepare a proper defense, it is imperative to fully understand the charge against you. Read the Code Section. Know the case law concerning your charge. If you want a good outcome on your case, you need to know the enemy you are facing. Only then can you develop an effective strategy.

CHAPTER 3

APPRECIATE THE CONSEQUENCES

THE SCARIEST PART OF GETTING A TRAFFIC TICKET IS fear of the consequences. Once you know your charge, you will be better able to understand the potential consequences for a traffic conviction. The difference between a traffic infraction (speeding, for example) and a misdemeanor (reckless driving, for example) is massive. This chapter will set out the potential punishments from worst to best.

No one wants to go to jail. I have had several potential clients crying on the phone, afraid that they may go to jail for getting a speeding ticket. But their fear was misplaced. Drivers charged with traffic infractions have no reason to fear jail. Those charged with misdemeanors, however, have reason for concern. Virginia Code Section 18.2-11 sets the maximum punishments for misdemeanors, such as reckless driving, driving under the influence, or driving on a suspended license. A judge can sentence a defendant up to twelve months in jail for a class 1 misdemeanor conviction, such as the charges mentioned in the last sentence. If you are convicted of a class 2 misdemeanor, you could get up to six months in jail, for a charge like no driver's license. Needless to say, if you have a traffic ticket with a possibility of jail time, you should strongly consider hiring a lawyer to help you.

Another significant consequence of some misdemeanor charges is a suspension of your license to drive in Virginia. A conviction for driving under the influence or reckless driving can call for a Virginia license suspension. Imagine not being able to drive for six to twelve months! You may say, "I am not licensed in Virginia, so it will not affect me." On the contrary, if you have a valid license in another state but lose your right to drive in the Commonwealth of Virginia, you could be charged with driving on a suspended license if you are caught driving in the state. Additionally, your own state may suspend your license based on a system of reciprocity.

The next consequence for convictions of either infractions or misdemeanors is fines. For a class 1 misdemeanor, in addition to a potential twelve month jail sentence, you could be fined up to $2,500.00. For class 2 misdemeanors, you could be fined up to $1,000.00. For class 3 misdemeanors, you could be fined up to $500.00. And for class 4 misdemeanors, you could be fined up to $250.00. As you can see misdemeanors are expensive. Traffic infractions also come with set, statutory fine ranges as well.

Traffic convictions can add points to your driving record. In Virginia, the best driving record you can obtain is a +5. If you get convicted of a traffic ticket, the convictions will bring your driving points down. Virginia Code Section 46.2-492 sets the demerits system for the Commonwealth. "Serious traffic offenses," such as driving while intoxicated and reckless driving, get six negative points. So even if you have a perfect +5 record, one conviction will bring your record into the negative. What the Code calls "relatively serious traffic offenses" result in four negative points, charges such as speeding ten to nineteen miles per hour or following too closely. "Less serious" offenses garner three negative points. And the key to all of this is, if you are convicted of a misdemeanor in Virginia, even a traffic one, it will ALWAYS be on your criminal record. There is no mechanism in Virginia to expunge a conviction. Once you are found guilty, it will follow you wherever you go.

A consequence some people do not think about with these cases is the impact they have on employment. Military servicemembers or civil government employees with security clearances can lose their jobs if convicted of certain traffic offenses. When applying for jobs that require you to drive, a potential employer may not look favorably upon certain traffic convictions. Their caution stems from potential liability exposure resulting from negligent hiring if they knew, or had reason to know, that you had previous negative driving history.

A traffic ticket conviction can increase your insurance premiums. This point is, most often, the concern of the majority of drivers who get a ticket. Insurance is in the business of making money, not helping you. If you increase the risk that you may get in an accident, the insurance company is going to increase your premium because they do not want to pay out to a victim of a personal injury case (trust me, as a personal injury lawyer too, I can verify that). Unlike our current healthcare, where people are getting reasonably priced insurance for preexisting conditions, there is no such mandate for drivers with preexisting traffic convictions. If you are convicted, and do not take steps to mitigate the situation, your insurance will increase.

While there may be other consequences for a conviction, these are the ones regularly experienced by Virginia drivers. They rank from severe (jail) to minor (increased insurance cost), but none of them are pleasant. Again, you certainly have the right to represent yourself. But with these potential punishments looming, hiring an attorney is in your best interest.

CHAPTER 4

PRACTICAL GUIDANCE FOR YOUR COURT APPEARANCE

TAKE A BREAK FROM THE WEIGHT OF THE LAW regarding your traffic case and, instead, turn your attention to some practical things to help your case. How should you dress for court? How should you address the court? What should you be doing while you are waiting in the courtroom?

Do any of these things really matter for my case? You bet they do!

Remember, cases are decided by a judge based on the evidence and the credibility of witnesses. The judge has never met you. He or she knows nothing about you, other than what will be presented in a five to seven minute hearing. But the judge will know the officer. The officer will likely have appeared numerous times before the judge. The judge will already have tested the credibility of the officer. With such little time to evaluate, you do not want to do anything that will reflect negatively on you before the court.

First impressions matter. We all know that from job interviews. People make snap judgments based on something as simple as whether a shirt is tucked in or hanging loosely. If a skirt is too short, people will judge. Fair or unfair, it is just the truth. Since a judge is just another person who happens to be wearing a robe, the judge is not immune to first impressions. So dress as if you are going to a job interview or an Easter Sunday service. Make sure the colors are conservative. No big designs or pictures. Do not wear shorts! You may not be even allowed into most courtrooms in shorts. Dress and groom yourself like you think an innocent person or someone who should be given consideration should look.

When you are addressing the court, make sure that you stand before talking, unless specifically directed otherwise by the court. Stand up straight, do not slouch, and do not cross your arms or put your hands in your pockets. When you speak to the judge, address the judge as "Your honor." Do not say "yeah" or "uh-huh." Say "yes" or "no," your honor. When the judge speaks, stop talking immediately, even if you are mid-sentence. Few things aggravate a judge more than feeling like she is having to talk over another person in her courtroom.

When testifying or asking questions of witnesses, remember the first rule: be polite and cooperative. Do not argue with witnesses when you should be only asking questions. Do not yell or show frustration. These attitudes suggest a lack of credibility. Instead, remain calm, cool, and collected. Present your case with boldness but humility. Even if you are ultimately found guilty, a positive demeanor can result in a much more favorable disposition than if you are crotchety.

In today's world, people take cell phones with them everywhere. Most courts, however, do not allow citizens to bring cell phones into the courthouse. If you do, they will either take them or instruct you to take the phone back to your car. If you have evidence on your phone the court needs to see, then you should immediately inform the bailiffs at the entrance of the courthouse of that fact. Generally, they will take possession of the phone and have it sent up to the courtroom to await your trial.

Want to know one of the best uses of your time while you are waiting in the courtroom? Pay attention! In most courts, judges will call first cases that have retained counsel (yet another reason to hire a lawyer – less wait time). But if you are set on representing yourself, watch the lawyers as they handle the case. Listen to how they enter pleas of guilty, not guilty, or no contest. Hear what the judge has to say about cases similar to yours. The lawyer will ask the judge for a particular remedy and provide for you some ideas about what to ask the court to do in your case. Sure, you could bring in the latest novel. But you would have to agree your time is better spent observing how you might improve your court situation. Take a note pad and pen with you and make notes of arguments the lawyers make or things that appear to annoy the judge. This small piece of advice can reap significant benefits in your case.

CHAPTER 5

DO YOU HAVE TO GO TO COURT FOR YOUR CASE?

"DO I HAVE TO GO TO COURT?" THIS QUESTION IS probably the one most asked by potential traffic clients. An attorney should be able to advise whether you need to appear if you retain his or her services. But if you plan to represent yourself, you need to know whether your appearance in court is either required or could be helpful. This chapter will examine the general rules, as well as the potential consequences, should you decide not to attend your court date.

As I mentioned in chapter 2, your required appearance depends on whether your charge is an infraction or a misdemeanor. In almost every misdemeanor case (with a few rare exceptions), you must appear. The reason, of course, is because you face the potential of jail time. The court cannot sentence you to jail without you being there (that pesky Constitution). You may say, "Well, if I could go to jail, then I don't want to go to court." Unfortunately, this kind of thinking may result in more problems. Virginia Code Section 19.2-128 makes it a crime to fail to appear. If you are charged with a misdemeanor offense, and fail to appear in court, the court can issue a capias (arrest warrant) for your failure to appear. This capias is an additional misdemeanor, meaning you could get up to an additional twelve months and another $2,500.00 fine. Ouch! The moral of the story is, if you are charged with a misdemeanor and have not hired an attorney, do not miss your court date.

Simple traffic infractions are another story. You are not required to appear for simple traffic infractions. You essentially have three options. First, you can prepay most all traffic infractions. Virginia Code Section 46.2-787.3 allows for prepayment of certain offenses and sets out the fine structure for such payments. But the trick is, paying your ticket does not make it go away. It does not get dismissed by your prepayment. By prepaying, you are actually pleading guilty to the charge. And if you were in an accident, your prepayment can have ramifications for any civil claim, including personal injury or property damage claims. Because prepaying is a guilty plea, you can expect your insurance to be notified as well. Clearly, this option is not great.

The second option is to simply do nothing. Since you are not required to appear for your infraction charge, you can just decide to not show up and not prepay. Virginia Code Section 19.2-258.1 grants you this option. If you fail to enter a written or court appearance, the court will find that you waived your hearing and the case will be tried in your absence. How do you think that trial will go? Unless you are one of the few where the officer does not show up for court, you are likely to be found guilty *in absentia*, which means guilty in your absence. While not the same as a guilty plea, it has the same effect on your driving record, points, and insurance. The court will notify you of the result of the case and send you a bill to pay your fines and court costs. This result is not great either.

The final, and best, option is to hire an attorney for your infraction. If you hire an attorney for an infraction, you are not required to appear and the lawyer can fight for you. If the officer does not show, your lawyer can ask for a dismissal. If the officer or other witnesses do appear, the attorney can cross-examine witnesses in a trial as if you were present. If the court finds evidence sufficient for you to be found guilty, the lawyer can ask the court to consider a reduction or a dismissal upon you completing certain requirements. Thus, you are not limited to the all or nothing approach of deciding not to appear or to prepay. A lawyer can give you options you would not otherwise have available. Thus, this option serves as the best opportunity for you to avoid wasting a day in court and getting a better outcome.

Even if you hire a lawyer, however, there may be some occasions where your appearance, though not required, may be beneficial. For example, if you are trying to claim that the officer made a mistake, the lawyer may suggest that you appear. While a lawyer can represent you at trial, he or she cannot testify as a witness for you. So if you have evidence you believe may conflict with the testimony of the officer, you may need to appear to testify. Additionally, in some jurisdictions, courts look favorably upon Defendants who are willing to take the time to come to court with a lawyer. An attorney should be able to advise you of this possibility. While no one wants to take off work for a whole day to sit in a courtroom, it may be beneficial for you and your lawyer to appear.

CHAPTER 6

GUILTY OR NOT GUILTY? THAT IS THE QUESTION!

IT'S GAME DAY. YOU HAVE BEEN PATIENTLY WAITING FOR the court to call your case. Finally, you hear your name. The bailiff waives at you to come to the front of the courtroom. You stand behind the table. Across from you stands the officer behind her table. Depending on the type of case, she may be joined by a member of the Commonwealth Attorney's office. The judge looks in your direction and asks, "Defendant, how do you plead? Guilty? Not guilty? Or no contest?" When the lights are shining on you, it is easy to freeze, like a child standing in the spotlight at the school play. How should you plead? What will happen in the courtroom based on your choice? Are there any ramifications for this decision beyond this traffic ticket hearing? This chapter will address each of these questions so you will be able to make an informed decision on your day in court.

When it comes to pleading not guilty, understand that you do not have to be innocent. You are, actually, presumed innocent throughout the pendency of the trial unless, or until, the Commonwealth Attorney is able to prove your guilt beyond a reasonable doubt. The Commonwealth is not, however, required to prove guilt beyond all doubt or any possible doubt. But just because you were actually speeding 70 mph in a 55 mph zone does not necessarily mean the officer has the evidence to prove your guilt beyond a reasonable doubt. In most cases, they do; but better to know before you plead.

At any rate, if you plead not guilty, the court will prepare for a trial. Because the Commonwealth has the burden of proof beyond a reasonable doubt, they have to present their evidence first. The officer can only testify to what he or she physically saw or heard. The officer does not have the right to testify about what someone else saw or heard, unless there is an exception to the rules of evidence on hearsay. If an officer tries to testify to something beyond what he or she actually saw or heard, you should object. Likewise, if an officer tries to give an opinion beyond what he or she saw or heard, you should object. After the officer is done testifying, you have the right to cross-examine the officer. Cross-examining the witness means you get to ask the officer questions about your case. You do not get to make statements to the officer. You do not get to argue with the officer. Cross-examination is only for questions of the officer.

After you are done cross-examining the officer, the court will ask if you want to testify. But before you say yes, are you sure the officer presented enough evidence of your guilt? If not, you should make a motion to strike at the conclusion of the officer's evidence, asking the court to dismiss the case. If the court agrees with your motion, the judge will dismiss the case. If the judge disagrees with your motion to strike, then you will have to decide whether to testify or not. You are NOT required to testify. You have a constitutional right to remain silent, even at the trial.

Should you choose to put on evidence, you will then be put under oath (if not done so at the beginning of the trial). You can then explain to the judge what happened and the facts regarding why you should not be found guilty. Here are some bad arguments often given for why you should be found not guilty:

1. I was just following the flow of traffic.

2. There was a car blocking the officer's ability to put his radar on my car.

3. The officer did not read me my rights.

4. I was just following my GPS.

There are many more similar arguments. Speeding cases in Virginia rarely result in not guilty verdicts. Reckless driving cases are actually easier to get not guilty verdicts than speeding cases, in my experience. After the conclusion of your evidence, the court will let you know if you have been found guilty or not guilty. If you are found not guilty, you get to leave. If you are found not guilty, then you need to stick around for sentencing (which will be addressed in the next chapter).

If you plead guilty, you are admitting that you committed the offense and that the Commonwealth need not put on a trial. If you plead guilty, the court will ask you some questions to make sure that your plea is made freely and voluntarily and that you understand the nature and consequences of the plea. If you plead guilty, there will be no trial. You waive your right to confront and cross-examine witnesses. You waive your right against self-incrimination, as well as the right to defend yourself. The court will ask the officer to summarize the evidence against you. After receiving the officer's summary, the court will find you guilty. Sentencing will follow.

The no contest plea trips most people up, because many have never heard of it. A no contest plea means that you are not contesting the evidence the officer would present, but you are not admitting your guilt. Technically, it is a plea of "nolo contendere," but hardly any judges use this term (probably because no one is sure how to pronounce it). But you should know, for all practical purposes, this plea has the effect of a guilty plea. The officer will summarize the evidence, rather than having a trial, and you waive the same rights you would waive under a guilty plea.

Why so much time explaining the differences of how to plead? Well, besides the aggravation it causes a judge when the Defendants do not understand the difference, how you plead has enormous implications outside of this trial; particularly if you were in an motor vehicle accident as a result of this traffic ticket. Under Virginia Code Section 8.01-418, a plea of guilty or nolo contendere (no contest) is admissible in a civil proceeding (personal injury claim or property claim) if the ticket "arose out of the same occurrence upon which the civil action is based." So if your accident resulted in someone getting injured in a motor vehicle accident, the victim's attorney will be able to tell the jury that you pleaded guilty or no contest to the very offense that caused their injuries. How do you think that will work out for you? But, if you pleaded not guilty, the jury will not hear about the traffic case even if the court finds you guilty. As you can see, the question about how you should plead has significant implications for your traffic case and beyond.

CHAPTER 7

IMPROVE YOUR OUTCOME

IF YOU HAVE BEEN FOUND GUILTY, THE COURT'S NEXT step will be to sentence you. The court has every right to sentence you to the maximum punishment allowable by statute for your offense. So what you are going to do to keep that from happening? What steps can you take to make you look redeemable to the judge? Once you know what those steps are, how can you complete them? And once they are completed, how should it be presented and argued to the court? This chapter will answer these questions and provide you the information to give your traffic case a makeover.

Right off the bat, you need to know that no Virginia traffic court treats traffic outcomes exactly the same. Some courts will accept some of these improvements to your case, while other courts prefer some of the other improvements. If you are not sure how your court will treat your case, your best bet is to complete and provide all of these improvements. Of course, doing so will take a great deal of time, which is why hiring an experienced Virginia traffic attorney may be your best option.

Nevertheless, these case improvements will certainly not harm your case and will likely benefit you at the sentencing.

The first thing you will need to bring with you is a driving record. The court is going to look at your driving history to determine if you are a danger to the roads or if this case was a minor "speed bump" in your life. Some courts only want to see your traffic history the last five years. Other courts want to see your full driving history. The best place to get your driving record is with your state Department of Motor Vehicles (DMV). Most DMVs will let you get your driving record online. There are some background check companies that provide driving records, but some courts do not accept those as reliable. If your record is good, the court will give it strong consideration. If your record is poor, then you have an uphill climb in getting a good result. But either way, courts generally require you present your driving history.

Another improvement to your traffic situation may be completing a driver improvement school course. The Virginia Department of Motor Vehicles has a list of Virginia-approved courses you can choose from, including in-person and online. Most courts require the driver to have the original certificate of completion sent to the court, so do not hire a company that will only email you a copy. Ensure that they will get the original to the court. Additionally, some courts want to order your completion of the class prior to your taking it. The reason is you may get a double benefit if you take it voluntarily and obtain positive points, while then using the voluntary class to get your ticket reduced in court.

So in some cases, I advise that the driver wait until the court orders the course to complete it. Again, this varies based on the jurisdiction of your case. If you have a clean record, most courts will consider dismissing the case upon your completion of driver improvement and payment of court costs, so long as your ticket is not egregious. But even if the court will not dismiss the case, presenting proof of completion of driver improvement will put you in a better position to get a reduction of your charge or, at minimum, a better outcome to some degree.

Depending on the vehicle you were driving, you may consider getting your speedometer checked to see if the speed was off. You can take your car to a body shop and they will test to see if your speedometer was a few miles per hour off than actual speed. Even if it is just a couple miles per hour off, a calibration can increase the chance for you to prevent points from being added to your record. Do an online search for "speedometer calibrations near me" and let them know you are getting a calibration for court. They will provide a notarized certificate showing the speedometer speed against the actual speed. This original calibration is what most courts will require to grant you a reduction. In other words, a copy is usually insufficient.

In some cases, especially high speed and reckless driving cases, a court may look favorably upon the completion of community service. First, you need to understand what community service is not. Community service is not doing extra work at your job. It is not doing work for a private company. Most courts require community service be for a non-profit that benefits the public that you are not already involved in. Examples of nonprofits might be United Way, Habitat for Humanity, or a soup kitchen. An example of government community service is washing fire trucks. When you do volunteer work, make sure that the supervisor keeps a log of your time and provides a letter to the court (again, not a copy) detailing the work you did and how you performed. The larger the number of hours the better positioned you will be for a better outcome.

If you are in the military, make sure you bring proof of your service. Some courts view military service favorably in traffic dispositions. If you are a student, bring a copy of your transcripts so the court can see your grades. The better the grades, the more responsible you will appear to the court. If you are employed, bring proof of employment and, perhaps, have your employer write a letter of commendation for the good work you have performed. You want the court to know that you are generally responsible and worthy of consideration for a reduction or dismissal.

CHAPTER 8

YOU PREPAID (OR FOUND GUILTY) – IS IT TOO LATE?

YOU ARE SITTING IN YOUR RECLINER WATCHING THE football game when, suddenly, you feel an ache in your stomach. No, it is not from the 20 chicken wings you just finished eating. You remember the court case for your ticket was set for Friday and you forgot about it. Panic ensues. You check the Virginia Judicial System website and realize the traffic court found you guilty in your absence. What do you do? Is it too late to have the ticket reduced? If not, how can you get the case back in front of a judge? This chapter will help you understand whether you still have the potential of getting your case before the court or if you are time-barred.

Whether you prepaid the ticket, were found guilty in your absence, or even if you went to court and were found guilty, you may still have the right to have your case heard again. The date of your sentencing in the traffic court starts the clock for these post-conviction remedies. It is crucial to keep up with this date, whether you intend to take action yourself or hire an attorney.

You have a right to appeal your traffic case from the Virginia district court to the Virginia circuit court where your traffic ticket was heard. The outcome of the district court case is irrelevant on appeal, because the circuit case hears the evidence *de novo*. You essentially get a do-over. The officer will have to come in and bring evidence against you, and you can present whatever evidence you have on your case anew. So if you did not have some of the evidence to improve your case from the previous chapter at the district court case, you can now present it to the circuit court judge for consideration. The trick is: you must note your appeal in writing within ten calendar days of the sentencing date. The only exception is when the tenth day falls on a weekend or holiday. In that event, you would have until the next day the court is opened. There is no jurisdiction to appeal if you miss this deadline. This is why keeping up with your court date is so important.

So what if you miss the appeal deadline? Are you out of luck completely? Fortunately, there is still hope. In the district courts, you can file a motion to reopen within sixty days of your traffic conviction. The Motion to Reopen/Motion to Rehear/Motion for New Trial fillable form can be found online. You will need to provide the case number, conviction, and date of conviction. You also must give an explanation for why the case should be reopened. There is no guarantee that the court will reopen. If reopened, the case must be heard by the same judge who heard the trial originally. If the court does not reopen the case, there is no basis to appeal that ruling.

Each of these remedies is time sensitive and requires proper documentation. Any mistake could potentially sabotage your ability to get back in court. You should not try to "wing it." Instead, you should hire an experienced Virginia traffic attorney to make sure that all the "i's" are dotted and "t's" are crossed.

ABOUT THE AUTHOR

ANDREW R. (DREW) PAGE IS AN ATTORNEY AND CO-owner of Randall | Page, P.C. in Suffolk, Virginia. Drew has successfully defended thousands of traffic cases. Over the past decade, Drew has represented politicians, other lawyers, judges, and an NFL coach for their traffic cases. He has served as an adjunct professor of trial practice, advanced trial practice, and legal research and writing at Regent University School of Law. While teaching at Regent, he coached two national trial championship teams. Drew served as the president of the Suffolk Bar Association and he has presented at a Virginia CLE program and has had several articles published in legal publications.

RANDALL | PAGE, P.C

143 N MAIN ST
SUFFOLK, VA 23434

PHONE: 757-935-9065

FAX: 757-935-9067

WA

Made in the USA
Monee, IL
24 March 2021

63666031R00022